Family Series **higher education**

Contents

Introduction	4
Choosing a University or College	8
Being away from home	10
Being a student	18
Ordering your priorities	23
What church?	27
What about the prodigal?	31
A final word	34

Introduction

Learning, training, and education beyond fifth or sixth form at school are increasingly necessary to prepare young people for employment in the technological, competitive, changing world in which we live. For some, this learning and training will be obtained in the course of their employment, but for many it will mean becoming full time students on a formal course of higher education at a university, or further education at a college. Government policy over the past forty years or so has encouraged young people to seek qualifications from these institutions, and now many thousands of students each year enrol for courses. This often involves them living away from home, and it will also mean that many of them go on to experience a higher level of education than their parents were able to enjoy.

Thousands of students each year enrol for courses

It is useful to look back briefly to note how all this has come about. The Industrial Revolution of the nineteenth century had drawn hundreds of thousands of people from the countryside into the burgeoning industries. For more than a hundred years it then became common practice for son to follow father into the same employment. Coal mines, steel works, textile mills, engineering workshops and shipyards saw generations of the same families pass through the ranks of employees. This led to communities being homes to many generations of the same families, often employed by the same employer, and content with, or at least resigned to, a life style which would not change. As a result, sons and daughters did not normally

Family Series **higher education**

the john ritchie
family series

let's talk about HIGHER EDUCATION

Copyright © 2000 John Ritchie Ltd. 40 Beansburn, Kilmarnock, Scotland

ISBN No. 0 946351 94 5

All rights reserved. No part of this publication may be reproduced in any form or by any means without prior permission of the copyright owner.

leave home until they married, and even then they would only move within their own area when accommodation became available. The thought of going to technical college or university must have been an unrealisable dream for many.

This had an interesting spiritual effect. In one place, the next generation of believers in a family was able to carry on the work of their Christian mothers and fathers. In many areas we still hear of families who were associated with the work of the gospel over a number of generations, so that sometimes the local people, instead of calling believers "Christians", called them by a name derived from the family name, so closely were they identified with the Christian work they did.

But change in society had to come, and for many, it was traumatic and sudden. For thousands of workers and for many leaders of

industry the pace of change and the reasons for it were beyond their understanding. They stood back bemused and uncomprehending as the industries which had been their life, and the lives of their fathers and

The decline of traditional industries was unstoppable

mothers, died. The decline of these traditional industries was unstoppable, due in some cases to a pool of cheaper labour becoming available in previously undeveloped countries. The march of the new technologies, which made obsolete many prized skills gained over long years of hard work and experience, was hard to accept.

For young people all this created a new situation, and opened up a new opportunity. Higher Education and Further Education became an accepted "must" for many families who previously would never have considered this as an option. The turning point come in the 1960's when great emphasis was placed on the expansion of universities and colleges of further education.

Within education itself a significant change was also taking place. It was the abandonment of any Christian or Biblical foundation on which the curriculum had been based for about a hundred years. This reflected changes in society, and has also accelerated that change. So nowadays in schools, rather than any Bible-based teaching, "multi-faith" and comparative religion lessons are common, along with humanistic and atheistic philosophies as a basis for everything. In the more mature environment of college or university some students may be required to listen to lectures or take part in debates the declared purpose of which is to deny the faith of the Bible. In some courses the student must also be prepared to study subjects containing elements which are quite opposed to Biblical teaching. Christian teenagers may find themselves taught by lecturers of atheistic or agnostic persuasions whose views are reflected strongly in what they teach, irrespective of the subject. This may not be true at all times, indeed it may be found that some lecturers are believers who will be both understanding and helpful to Christian students facing such problems.

Student years are formative and impressionable

The student years are formative and impressionable years. The new environment in which you live, the diverse views and opinions which you will meet, and the fact that you may be away from home for the first time, make this a crucial period in life. Great care will need to be taken in assessing what you hear and in rationalising what you are taught. You will also have to be careful in deciding what company you keep and what spiritual home you choose from the many "Christian" organisations and bodies to be found in the student environment. A young believer coming from a sheltered background will find his or her faith and beliefs challenged, and at the same time experience greater freedom to act than had been allowed at home. How these challenges are met and how this freedom is used may set your course for a lifetime.

Clearly your student years are critical years for you - don't waste them or misuse them! Many people in later life look back upon their student days and the place they studied with fondness and gratitude, because it was then and there that their lives were shaped, their character established, their convictions deepened, their outlook became balanced, true friendships were made, as well as their career opened up.

Critical years for you - don't waste or misuse them!

Choosing a university or college

Before leaving school, the choice of a university or college is very important for you. You need to look carefully into what is available, once you have identified the course which you wish to take. Your task meantime surrounds the relatively simple matter (?) of working hard to obtain the passes and the grades which you need, to achieve acceptance by the institution which has the reputation of offering the best to suit your requirements. This is a very important part of the process. You may, however, end up having to accept the offer of a place that is not your first choice, but if it will lead to the degree or the qualifications that you seek, or even if you get your first choice, is there any other issue of importance to consider?

An important issue

"Not forsaking the assembling of yourselves together" (Heb 10.25).

Take into account your spiritual development

There is one other matter which is important - of equal importance with the other factors involved in your choice. As a believer you must take into account your spiritual development as well as your academic development. You must not enter this stage of your education thinking that you can put your spiritual life on hold for a number of years, and then take it up again once your studies are over. Years in higher or further education are not a holiday period from the responsibilities of spiritual life. If you think and act like this, your spiritual growth will be stunted at a vital stage in your development. You will find at the end of your studies that any appetite which you had for the Scriptures has gone, and with it will have disappeared any desire to take up where you left a few years earlier.

The exhortation of the Word of God, to "not forsake the assembling of ourselves together", is as relevant to the student as it is to all other Christians. If you consider that this is too much to ask of overburdened students, remember that the teaching of the Word of God applies to every phase of life and never asks us to do the impossible.

The local church

It is vital, therefore, to make enquires regarding a local church to which you can be commended as you leave home, and with which you will be in fellowship during your student days. If an offer of a student place is made to you from an area where no proper local church fellowship would be possible, an alternative place should really be sought, looking to the Lord to guide you.

Many local churches in college or university towns have, over the years, worked hard to make young folk feel at home and have provided the spiritual atmosphere that is necessary for Christian growth. They have welcomed generations of teenagers, and the elders have years of experience in guiding young believers who find themselves away from home. The spiritual anchor which this provides, and the friendship and guidance which is offered, can turn a lonely town or city, full of alluring temptations, into a place which will be fondly remembered as one of warm Christian fellowship where teaching was received and impressions made which helped to build Christian character. To find the right area and the right local church it may be necessary to make careful enquiries or even to visit an area with this sole purpose in mind. This would be time well spent.

Being away from home

So you have now been accepted for a university place! The prospect of leaving home, or at least loosening the ties of home and enjoying some more freedom, beckons invitingly. You are a believer and have been participating in the work of the local church, but it will be good to move to pastures new. Listen to some good advice from the Scriptures.

Remember what you have been taught.

"My son, forget not my law" (Prov 3.1).

There may be a temptation to think that what you were taught at home and in your local church is a very restrictive view of Christian life. In this you will not be alone. There has always been a temptation to underestimate the value of what has been received in the home area. The prodigal son of Luke 15 made the same mistake.

You need to remember that, as a believer, you have a standard by which you can judge all that you hear and see. This standard, the Bible, has stood the test of time and survived many assaults. It must more than ever become your handbook in the years ahead. You will meet criticism and scepticism, but you must keep the Book as your main reference work. If you do so you will find, as countless others have, that, amazingly, the Book is relevant and reliable, and the teaching found in its pages is practical and workable in modern society. Make university or college the place where you put the Scriptures to the test and you will find just how reliable they are. The advice of Solomon is still sound today, "Trust in the Lord with all thine heart; and lean not unto thine own understanding. In all thy ways acknowledge Him, and He shall direct thy paths" (Prov 3.5-6).

Do not be tempted to stray.

"*My son, if sinners entice thee, consent thou not*" (Prov 1.10).

For the first time you may come into extensive contact with many young people who are not believers and who may know nothing of the teaching of the Bible. Their lifestyle may seem, at first, to be very attractive. These new friends seem to enjoy themselves in ways which you were always taught were unacceptable, and yet they appear to be happy and satisfied with life.

In this new "exciting" environment temptation will not be long in coming. The lack of restraint and the "freedom" which is now yours will open doors to behaviour and to beliefs which are new and seem inviting. There will be those who are prepared to entice you and introduce you into new "experiences". How harmless they appear to be and what excitement they promise!

Temptation will not be long in coming

It is at times like these that you need to listen again to the advice of Proverbs 1. Stop and think! Do not rush into something which may affect the whole of your future life! You may be standing at the crossroads. It may be the most important decision you have to make since your decision to accept the Lord Jesus as your Saviour. Any thought that there is no harm in trying this or that, just to see what it is like, should be banished. When sin comes calling, the issues are never trivial.

The issues are never trivial

What may seem particularly attractive about this new life style which you are witnessing is that it has no barriers or "no go" areas. New experiences are there to develop your character, you are told, new thrills and pleasures to bring enjoyment into your days and new views of life which fascinate! Take care! The Adversary never places temptation in front of you which does not seem to be attractive. In the Garden of Eden the promise that Adam and Eve would be as gods seemed to open up to them new and exciting possibilities. The terrible disaster which followed is a warning to all who ignore the guidance of Scripture.

Make an early declaration of your faith.

Many problems can be avoided by ensuring that from the beginning of your student life you make it known that you are a Christian. If you fail to do this and start to accompany unbelievers in their social activities you will find it very difficult to make a break. As time goes on you may well lose the will to let it be known that you are a Christian and indeed may well be so compromised that you find it impossible to witness for the Lord Jesus.

If, however, you witness for the Lord from the beginning you will find that others will not want you to join them in their social life. The last thing that the world desires is the company of true believers. You will find that the pathway of separation from the world is not only your wish, but also theirs. They will encourage your path of separation by their refusal to bring you into their company. You must not regard this as "rejection" by others, but rather see it alongside the teaching of the Word of God. It will be a further incentive to help you find your friends among Christians and spend your time with them.

In student life you will mix with all kinds of other young people. A unique opportunity is yours of witnessing to them. Some will have their minds made up and may at first scorn your beliefs - but later respect you for them. Others, however, will have open minds, as they too will be away from earlier influences over their lives. They may wish, even from curiosity, to listen to what you have to say, and become interested. Of course how you say it matters. The words of 1 Peter 3.15 are a constant challenge: "Be ready always to give an answer to every man that asketh you a reason of the hope that is in you with meekness and fear". Over many years Christian students have had the privilege of leading other students to faith in Christ by both living a righteous life and quietly witnessing to them as opportunities arise. God may use you in this way if you are willing and ready.

God may use you if you are willing and ready

Two good examples to follow
Joseph

"Joseph being seventeen years old, was feeding the flock with his brethren" (Gen 37.2).

Joseph was a young man of seventeen when he found himself away from home, but in company which appeared to be "safe". He is with his brothers and they are tending the family flocks. One would have thought that little trouble or temptation would come to Joseph in such an environment, but it did come from this most unexpected quarter. We do not know the details of what took place but it is clear that the conduct of his brothers, away from the restraint of the family home, left much to be desired. Joseph did not take part in this sinful activity and when he returned home he reported the situation to his father. He did not do this out of unworthy motives. He could have made life easier for himself by remaining quiet, but by so doing he may have become implicated in these sad events. He felt that it was necessary to report the matter, no doubt with the good of his brothers in mind. He understood that conduct away from home should not be unprincipled, and the standards which he had learned had to be honoured no matter where he was. This stand which he took was an early indication of the faithfulness to God which characterised all his future life.

The standards he had learned had to be honoured

Joseph was later sold as a slave into Egypt far away from home, in a foreign land where several great tests and temptations were to reach out to him. First, he was tested by sexual appeal; second, he was tested by adversity; and third, he was tested by prosperity. Students may find themselves tested in these same ways and it is salutary to learn from the experience of Joseph.

Joseph refused - definitely and repeatedly

Potiphar's wife was unprincipled and immoral. She was determined to enter into a sexual relationship with Joseph and deliberately brought about a situation where they were alone together. Joseph refused her. He said No! - definitely and repeatedly. His final resort in fleeing from the situation, despite the difficulties which followed, is a good example of how to handle such circumstances.

Student life offers opportunities of casual and protracted encounters with those of the opposite sex. Flirting and much more are commonplace. The believer knows well that this behaviour is condemned in the Scriptures and circumstances do not provide excuses. Do not act in a way which you will regret for years to come. Beware of situations which facilitate entering into relationships of this nature, and take care not to send out any "signals" that such an approach as Potiphar's wife made would be welcome.

He did not become bitter by the turn of events

Joseph was tested by adversity. He was imprisoned, but in spite of this he did not become bitter by the turn of events. Having acted righteously he was content to leave matters in the hand of the Lord. There will be times when, as a student, you will feel that things are not going well. You have sought to live according to the Word of God, but this has not led to the success which you expected. Other students who have gone in for all the pleasures of the world seem to be successful, but you are not. You have applied yourself seriously to your studies, but at the moment things do not look too good. What is the answer? Like Joseph, continue as you have started, persevere with your work, and leave the issues in the hand of the Lord.

Family Series **higher education**

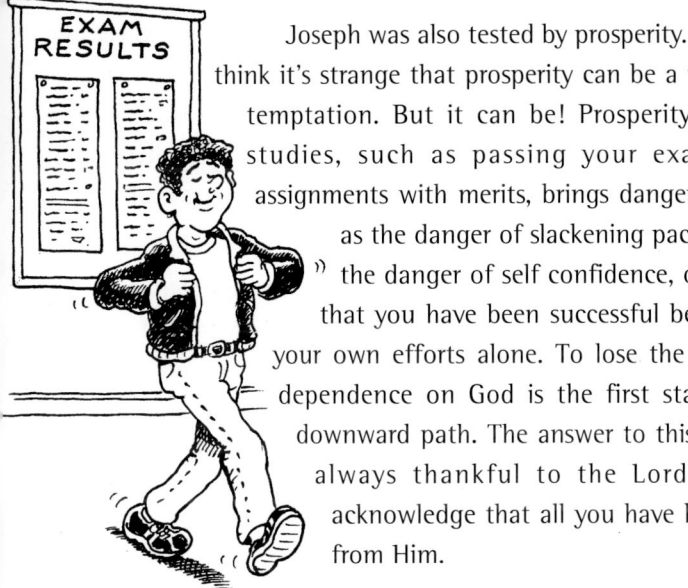

Joseph was also tested by prosperity. You may think it's strange that prosperity can be a means of temptation. But it can be! Prosperity in your studies, such as passing your exams and assignments with merits, brings danger. As well as the danger of slackening pace there is the danger of self confidence, of feeling that you have been successful because of your own efforts alone. To lose the sense of dependence on God is the first stage on a downward path. The answer to this is to be always thankful to the Lord and to acknowledge that all you have has come from Him.

Be always thankful to the Lord

Daniel

"*But Daniel purposed in his heart that he would not defile himself with the portion of the king's meat*" (Dan 1.8).

The circumstances in which Daniel found himself were much less favourable than those of Joseph in the field with his brothers. He also was a young man when he and his companions were taken prisoners from the city of Jerusalem to the foreign city of Babylon - to a strange people with strange customs and surrounded by idolatry. The purpose of the king was, by education and custom, to change them from being Israelites into being Babylonians. The reality is that they were to go through a period of "higher education".

Their course of study may not appear to be similar to that of students today, but the purpose was. As a first step they were to be treated lavishly and given the same food as that which graced the king's table. This might be thought of as a great privilege, but Daniel and his friends realised that the food contravened the dietary laws found in the Scriptures. They, therefore, purposed that they would not eat this food - a dangerous thing to do in a foreign autocrat's court. We should not be surprised to learn that, when allowed the diet of their choice for a period of ten days, "their countenances appeared fairer and fatter in flesh than all the children which did eat the portion of the king's meat" (Dan 1.15). The result of their faithfulness to Scriptures was that they made more progress than the others.

Do not compromise your beliefs

At least three valuable lessons can be learned from the experience of Joseph and of Daniel and his friends. First, do not compromise your beliefs when in a strange place. Second, refusal to compromise may appear the difficult choice at first, but it is beneficial in the long run. Third, how you react to this early test of your beliefs may indicate how your future will turn out.

Another example - from which to turn away

"And Samson went down" (Judges 14.1).

Having considered examples of two good young men who found themselves away from home, we turn our attention to an example of a promising young man who took himself away from home.

Samson had begun to show promise that he would be a valiant servant of the Lord. "The Spirit of the Lord began to move him", and his early life indicated that he was a young man who had given himself over to obedience and devotion to the Lord who had blessed him. He was, however, a man who never did realise to the full the potential which he seemed to have, and the first indication of his weakness was seen on the first recorded occasion of his leaving home.

At that time he was probably about twenty years old, and in Timnath he saw one of the daughters of the Philistines. The attraction of the opposite sex was always to be a danger to Samson, and the Adversary was quick to put this temptation in his way at the earliest opportunity. Samson was unable to resist! When Joseph encountered an immoral woman who tried to tempt him, he fled. In a situation which was easier to control than Joseph's, Samson did not turn away, but rather pursued the attraction. Sadly, he was revealing the desires which would bring tragedy into his life.

In leaving home, or in mixing with others, you may meet the same type of attack as Samson. Beware of the wiles of the devil, who knows our weaknesses better than we know them ourselves. He will attempt to bring temptation before us which would compromise our testimony and destroy our future usefulness for God. The course on which you as a new student embark is not only an opportunity to show the reality of your faith, it is also a time of danger. Yielding to temptation can spoil a whole life, preventing it from fulfilling the early promise which it showed.

Yielding to temptation can spoil a whole life

Being a student

According to the dictionary, a student is, believe it or not, "one who studies"! But what kind of student will you be? Some students do become so interested and involved in their subjects that studying, reading, and researching absorbs all their time and energy. They are often called swots! Others take a different approach and are there for the social life, doing the minimum of work to scrape through and stay on the course. They are often called absentees, or even less polite names! Most students, however, are somewhere between these extremes, and you will need to think well about how your time as a student will be spent. What are you there for?

Notice first that if you put your mind to it, studying can be deeply satisfying and may become absorbing. Whatever your chosen subjects, the more you look into them, perhaps guided and motivated by an enthusiastic lecturer, the more you can find to interest you and challenge your mind in the best possible way. Remember if God in His goodness has given you a good brain and the capacity to think deeply, He intends you to use it and not waste it.

Insight from a spiritual and eternal perspective

But realise too that the way you look at things as a believer in the Lord Jesus may be a lot different from the way they are presented to you by tutors whose outlook on life is materialistic or atheistic. You have greater insight from a spiritual and eternal perspective. Someone said that Christians on their knees see farther than philosophers on their tiptoes! Do not become conceited or arrogant in this, but do think for yourself, always guided by the Scriptures whose truth is not governed by the latest research or has to be reinterpreted by current thinking. Many famous scientists and philosophers in the past have been humble believers in the truth of the Bible, and many current ones are too. Written above the doorway of a laboratory in an old university in the UK are the words, "The works of the Lord are great, sought out of all them that have pleasure therein" (Psa 111.2) - a reminder of how study used to be regarded - yours can still be!

At university or college a whole variety of extra-curricular activities will be available. Student societies exist for almost anything you like! During freshers' week you may be faced with dozens of invitations to join some club or society. For some young people this is what they want, and they hardly have time for lectures, far less for study, as they get caught up in endless meetings, outings, and the social life which goes with them. Other students simply lose direction and motivation and need no excuse for late night partying, late morning sleeping, repeated coffee breaks or visits to nearby taverns, and generally passing the rest of the time dreaming about it. Such students are a headache to their tutors, and most, sadly, give up or have their courses terminated. They have wasted their time, and the time and efforts of others who have tried to help them and motivate them.

Lose direction and motivation

Apply yourself to all the components of your course

So how are you going to tackle the freedom and the responsibility of your student life? First remember why you are there. If you have sought the Lord's guidance and help to get you there, you will want to make the most of the opportunities you are given. You wish to obtain some degree or qualification, and a course of study has been provided for you - at considerable public expense! So you must apply yourself to your studies, and tackle all the components of your course - including those you perhaps like least or find hardest.

Among other things this will require you to attend lectures and tutorials regularly. These are for your benefit, and whilst there are books in which you can read about your subject (and you should read these anyway), the best way to learn is by following the pace and direction of your lecturers who are there to help you. Don't miss tutorials either - they give you the opportunity to ask questions and seek more explanation if you need it. Lecturers actually like to be asked questions, and to see some interest from their students. Another habit you should try to get early on, is handing in work on time - whether it be reports, assignments, essays or anything else related to your course. By doing the work at the prescribed time you gain most benefit from it for yourself, and you assist the person who has to mark it and give you feedback from it. You also stand the best chance of obtaining good grades this way. Diligence in all your work is commended in Holy Scripture (Col 3.17,23).

Diligence in all your work is commended in Holy Scripture

As for private study, this is absolutely necessary. Attendance at classes is only part of your week's allocated tasks. As a general rule, you should allocate at least an hour to private study for every hour of formal class time you have, to give yourself a chance of success. Different people have different methods of study, but it is done most effectively alone, and with pen and paper to hand. You will have to share work with other students sometimes, and you should do that willingly and co-operatively - this will help your Christian testimony towards them. But never be tempted to hand in work for assessment which you have simply copied from others, as if it were your own - that is dishonest and anyway will be of no help to you.

Will you have any time for other things you want to do? Many students nowadays have to work part time to survive financially, and this eats into the week quite a bit. If you have to do that, be reasonable with yourself and do not try to do more than you can afford just so that you can keep up with others who seem to have cash to spare. For there is that most important aspect of your life which you simply must give time to - your own private time with the Lord, reading His Word and praying daily. Also the meetings of the local church call for your presence, for your own benefit and blessing and for your sharing in true fellowship with others. If you ever feel that these things are demanding too much of your time, just think how much more time some of your classmates spend on their chosen pursuits, their hobbies and sports. Yours are so much more worthwhile and satisfying.

Exams

Hardly anyone enjoys exams; likely you never did at school and you don't think you will at university or college either. There is no doubt they are stressful, for so much appears to depend on those two or three hour sessions of concentrated thought and writing. There is so much to try to remember and the questions are never the ones you expect!

But exams are part of the process of assessment of students' progress and ability, and have been for a long time. In many courses now they are a smaller component of the overall programme of performance testing and grading, but they still count and you must not treat them lightly, or wish they didn't exist. A course with no real hurdles or tests of ability would not be worth very much - anyone could enrol and get the piece of paper proclaiming their achievement, but achievement of what?

So how will you approach exams? First you must prepare yourself, and that cannot be done the night before or even the week before. If you have heeded the advice given above in diligently applying

Pray for the Lord's help

yourself to your studies and course tasks throughout the term or semester, you will already be well prepared. Some extra hours of concentrated study just before the exams will refresh your memory and sharpen your understanding to face these questions with some confidence. Remember that examiners are not trying to see how many people they can fail!

There is something else though which you as a believer can do, and it does help greatly. Pray for the Lord's help - especially to cope with examination nerves and anxieties. The words of 1 Peter 5.7 apply in all situations, including exams, "Casting all your care upon Him; for He careth for you". Prayer on its own will not give miracle passes in your exams, but if you have diligently done your part, the Lord will honour your faith and can give a confidence which is not available to many who may be more academically able than you are.

A good degree

"Study to shew thyself approved unto God" (2 Tim 2.15).

No doubt you wish to work for and obtain a good degree, one that you feel you have earned and which will open up the way ahead in your career. But there is another degree which every Christian student in every faculty should study for - not BA, MA, BSc or even PhD - it is AUG, "approved unto God".

Whatever you do with your life and particularly with your time as a student, never lose sight of the fact that as a believer you are responsible to your Lord and Saviour for all you do. In public before others or in private before God your life counts for something and each passing day can be used to please Him. These formative years as a student are so important for you that you dare not treat them lightly. You can carry forward with you something which will benefit you for the rest of your life, and through you benefit others, and at the end lead to the ultimate heavenly graduation award, "Well done, good and faithful servant!"

Family Series **higher education**

Ordering your priorities

Student life is usually the first time when adult responsibilities are faced and freedoms enjoyed. The need to order your priorities now is vital and, as we have seen, the decision as to how time is allocated is fundamental to your success. Ahead of you there is the prospect of studies which will make great demands on your time and will probably be more onerous than those which you have previously undertaken. In addition to this you are in a study environment which is very different from that which you experienced at school. You will be treated as an adult and it will be left to you to ensure that you tackle your tasks without having to be prodded into serious study.

How time is allocated is fundamental to success

But there will be other demands on your time and attention! The importance of your studies may so overwhelm you, and you may decide that your studies should take precedence over any other issue. But should they?

"Seek ye first the kingdom of God" (Matt 6.33).

The problem faced is one that will be present over the years to come, if the Lord will, and is not just a factor of student life. The Lord Jesus spoke of the many issues which face us all and summed them up as anxiety over "what ye shall eat, or what ye shall drink;... what ye shall put on" (Matt 6.25). He describes the concerns we have about earning a living and ensuring that we have the resources necessary for life. Higher Education and Further Education is part of that process, for you are fitting yourself to be able to meet these responsibilities. But there is the danger of concentrating on these demands and forgetting others!

The words of the Lord Jesus are quite clear: "But seek ye first the kingdom of God and His righteousness and all these things shall

"Seek ye first the kingdom of God"

be added unto you" (Matt 6.33). The first priority must be spiritual! This is not concentrating on spiritual matters and neglecting your studies, nor is it working at what you enjoy instead of applying yourself to what you may find less enjoyable. It is simply recognising the importance of developing what is most important, while applying yourself conscientiously to the studies in hand.

It is important to see that there is a promise in these words of the Lord Jesus: "All these things shall be added unto you". If we ignore His teaching here we may well achieve our educational objectives, but at what a cost! If we seek to put His words into practice He tells us that seeking the kingdom and satisfying our needs are not two opposing aims, they are complementary. On top of what we gain spiritually the other things will be "added" unto us. They will be an addition on top of what has greater importance. Those who pursue this course are doubly blessed.

"First gave their own selves to the Lord" (2 Cor 8.5).

Here is another "first" to which we must pay attention. The context here is one of giving to the work of the Lord. The churches of Macedonia had been generous in their giving to the fund which Paul had gathered to alleviate the poverty of the believers in Judaea. Despite their own relative poverty they had exceeded all that Paul had expected of them in their desire to help others. What pleased him even more, however, was that this giving was the outcome of lives which had been given firstly to the Lord. The Lord was put first in their lives and it showed.

The outcome of lives given firstly to the Lord

The subject which we are presently considering is not giving, but nevertheless the principle holds good in every area of life. If we first devote ourselves to the Lord it will be apparent by how we live. The Macedonians had their priorities right and give us all an example well worth following.

"If there be first a willing mind" (2 Cor 8.12)

Still dealing with the same subject of giving and laying down principles which are true at all times, Paul writes of the value of having a willing mind. When tackling spiritual work of any kind it is essential that we are willing to carry it out. As a student you must be willing to tackle your studies, but you must also be willing to pursue spiritual activities. Do not be the one who has to be dragged along, not even the one who is there simply because others involve you. One of the saddest things written about Lot was that when Abraham journeyed, Lot went with him (Gen 12.4;13.1;13.5). He had no direction in his own life which was the result of his own devotion to God. Rather he followed the footsteps of someone else. Even although he was following the footsteps of a great man of God it was not enough to preserve him from the disaster which overwhelmed him.

Education exercises the mind and keeps it occupied with detail which demands concentration. It is, however, possible to do this and have a mind which is willing to engage in the service of the Lord whenever it is possible so to do. Be known as one who is willing, not foolish and profligate with the use of your time.

Be known as one who is willing

"Honour the Lord...with the firstfruits of thine increase" (Prov 3.9).

What about your personal giving? Is it not well known that students have little money to spare and find it difficult enough to make ends meet without there being other demands on their precious resources? That is very true, and you are not expected to do what is not possible. But you can look at this as a challenge to put the Word of God to the test. Has the Lord not declared that if you bring all your tithes into the storehouse, He will open the windows of heaven and pour you out a blessing (Mal 3.10)?

Even when your resources are scarce it is always good practice to put the Lord first in this important area of Christian life. If you think that your resources are so small that they will be of no value in

His service you must think again. Remember that what you give to the Lord is not evaluated in heaven by the values of the world. The Lord Jesus stood one day in the Temple in Jerusalem and watched rich people cast into the treasury great sums of money. Into the temple came a poor woman who only had two mites. That was the sum total of her wealth, and she cast it all into the treasury. Those watching would regard her gift as worthless, but not so in heaven. The Lord Jesus declared that it was worth more than the gifts of the rich. Her gift was measured by the devotion which prompted it. Their gifts, vast in terms of the currency of earth, were worthless in heaven.

Adopt the practice of regular giving

Keep that in mind as you examine the little you have. Give what you can to the Lord. He values it when it is given out of devotion to him. In early life it is good to adopt the practice of regular giving. The Lord will be glorified and you will benefit.

Family Series **higher education**

What church?

Advice has already been given to ensure that a suitable local church is accessible for you, but the question to address is, "As a student what local church should I attend?" Even if the local church to which you have been commended is within easy travelling distance, will it not broaden experience and be a valuable part of the learning process to attend as many "fellowships" as possible? You might feel that the newly enjoyed freedom you have opens up possibilities which did not exist at home.

Amongst the range of activities and interests vying for the time and support of a new student, there will also be a broad, dazzling range of "Christian" activities. To the believer newly come from home, the possibilities may appear almost irresistibly inviting. At least four avenues open up to those who wish to have fellowship with other believers.

The possibilities may appear inviting

The options open to the student

The first is to have only a nominal connection with your local church. This will allow you to give the impression to parents and others that your spiritual life is healthy although there is no other spiritual activity apart from occasional attendance at the meetings. It may be that this attendance is more regular than what can be described as "occasional" but it hides the truth that there is little, if any, real interest.

The second is to mix attendance at the local church with involvement in other "Christian" groups and activities within and outwith the university. The attraction of this is that it will probably let you enjoy a wider circle of friendship and keep you very busy in a host of diverse activities. If you wish to direct your youthful vigour and energy along spiritual channels this may appear to provide "liberty" from "old fashioned restrictions". Are we not "all one in Christ Jesus" and would this breadth of fellowship not offer opportunities to serve in areas which are new and "exciting"? Is this not a grand opportunity to learn what others believe and to enter into new avenues of service?

The third is to abandon the local church completely. The reasons given may be that there are not enough young people there or that the church fellowship is small and old fashioned. Compared to other "fellowships" it appears to be unexciting and lacks the vibrant appeal which the student seeks. It may be that the Christians in fellowship in that church do not make the student feel welcome, although this would be an unusual situation in a university town. Maybe the grass seems greener elsewhere.

A place which will be your spiritual home

The fourth is to give all your effort to the local church of Scripture and concentrate all your spiritual activity to help its testimony and fellowship, to develop your spiritual life in a place which will be your spiritual home from home.

In examining these options we must remember that there are many believers working well and sincerely in different churches and organisations. As a student you will meet other young people full of enthusiasm for the Christian work in which they are engaged. When a young man or woman has a burning desire to witness to others, this enthusiasm can be very persuasive and lead us to believe that vigour and commitment must make a work worth supporting. This is particularly true when a student has come from a local church at home where tradition reigned in place of truth and where energy has given way to apathy.

Let us examine these options. In doing so we must remember

that the principles which hold for spiritual life at home are the same as those which hold for spiritual life when living away from home.

Deciding on the correct option

The first option, a "nominal" association with the local church, may appear attractive to those who feel that the student years should be a time of concentrating on secular studies and of leaving spiritual matters until these years are over. This is based on a view that the cost of discipleship is not worth paying when there are other legitimate interests to pursue. It will not do for those who have an interest in spiritual matters.

The second option is to engage is any area of activity which is classed as "Christian". Care must be taken in this. We must always obey the Scriptures. It will not be the desire of any spiritual young man or woman to disobey the Word of God while seeking to serve the One whom we claim to be our Lord.

Always obey the Scriptures

The third option of abandoning the local church because it does not appeal to you is a decision based purely on circumstances and personal feeling. It does not take the teaching of Scripture into account at all. It can only be a decision based on faulty spiritual reasoning which you will surely not wish to follow through.

The fourth option is to concentrate your efforts on the local church to which you have been commended. This is the best course of action to take! If the numbers are small, it is an opportunity to help and to gain valuable experience which will prove useful in future service. It will provide avenues of service which otherwise may never have opened up. It will mature your faith and give practical application of what you have been taught before. If the numbers are large, it is an opportunity to learn to co-operate in a larger group, taking the part for which you are gifted. Whether the numbers are small or large it is a teaching experience which can lay a firm foundation for the days ahead.

Church fellowship must always be where scriptural principles are obeyed

Essentially, as we have already said, the decision you make has to be based on exactly the same criteria which hold good at home or in any other situation. Student life does not absolve you from the responsibilities of discipleship, and church fellowship must always be decided on the basis of where scriptural principles are obeyed. For example, if headship in the church is not acknowledged by sisters refusing to cover their heads and remain silent during the meetings, scriptural principles are being set aside (see 1 Corinthians 11 and 14). Or if the charismatic movement has made inroads and there are claims to be speaking with "tongues" etc., the Word of God is being ignored in favour of guidance by "experience", which is always dangerous.

Family Series **higher education**

What about the prodigal?

It may be that this booklet is being read by a young man or woman who, although brought up in a Christian home, is not a believer. The opportunity to leave home and start a life elsewhere offers possibilities which you intend to explore with relish. You have listened to the gospel for years and have little interest in it or in the lifestyle of your parents. You may not make it known to them, but now you intend to make a break with all that is "Christian". The world lies out there to be enjoyed and you intend to do that to the full.

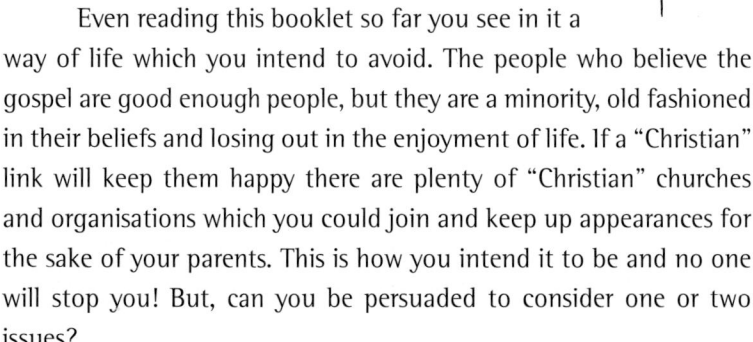

Even reading this booklet so far you see in it a way of life which you intend to avoid. The people who believe the gospel are good enough people, but they are a minority, old fashioned in their beliefs and losing out in the enjoyment of life. If a "Christian" link will keep them happy there are plenty of "Christian" churches and organisations which you could join and keep up appearances for the sake of your parents. This is how you intend it to be and no one will stop you! But, can you be persuaded to consider one or two issues?

A life without Christ is a wasted life.

"Wasted his substance with riotous living" (Luke 15.13).

The thought of "waste" would never have entered the mind of this young man who went out to enjoy the world. Enjoyment and excitement would be the two emotions which filled his mind. The future looked bright and inviting, without a cloud on the horizon.

Life without Christ is wasted.

But the verdict of Scripture is "waste", and even if "riotous living" is not on your agenda, the verdict remains the same.

Only one life lies before you

Only one life lies before you. The number of years is not known. Consider carefully, do you want to waste what God has given you? A Christian has the potential to live in a way which will bring blessing now and reward for eternity. To live otherwise is folly and waste. You may think that the Christian life is one in which much is lost. If that is how you think, listen to the words of Jim Elliot, a young American graduate who gave his all for the Lord, martyred in the jungles of Ecuador in January 1956 : "He is no fool who gives what he cannot keep to gain what he cannot lose".

A life without Christ is an empty life.

"He began to be in want" (Luke 15.14).

This may seem a strange statement to make. Does it really make sense to say it is empty in view of the great success stories which you see around? Surely there are many who have rejected the gospel, and could not be classed as poor?

True riches are not the riches of earth

True riches are not the riches of earth. "Treasure in heaven" is a reality. As time goes on the futility of life without the hope of the gospel will become obvious. You may try to shut it out by filling your life with activity, work and business, but you will not be successful. The stresses and cares of life will eventually take their toll and you will not have the resources which are available to the Christian. It is then that you will begin "to be in want". You will feel the poverty of your position. Like so many you may wish to turn to God in the crisis, but will this feeling of need simply disappear if and when the crisis passes?

A life without Christ is a life which demands a decision.

"And when he came to himself" (Luke 15.17).

Circumstances in the life of the prodigal sank to low ebb. In the midst of his trouble he "came to himself" and decided that he must return home. This, however, could only be done if he was prepared to admit that he had sinned. The turning point had been reached!

Is this not the time for you to make that decision? Starting out on this new phase of your life would be much more significant if it was also the occasion of you starting a new life as a Christian. You know the terms of the gospel and have often heard of the need to be saved and how to be saved. Delay is dangerous! Turn to the Saviour now!

Maybe you did profess to be saved when you were younger, but you have drifted away from any real commitment to Christ. You could be classed as a backslider, trying to forget about your earlier profession. However, if you were truly saved, you still belong to Christ and He longs for your return, and your heavenly Father longs to welcome you back. You never will be truly happy until you do return. All that you have just read about a wasted life and an empty life will be true of you if you do not. Make up your mind to return now!

Make up your mind to return

A final word

To enter Further Education or Higher Education is a privilege and must be treated responsibly. It is not an opportunity to be frittered away in time-wasting pursuits, nor has it to be lost by failing to work industriously. If advantage is not taken of the opportunity, regrets in later life are inevitable. Consider the thoughts of someone who treated education carelessly, and eventually sees those who were fellow students graduating and finding good employment, while they themselves are doing something which is much less rewarding and satisfying than what could have been. Do not finish your education with the words "if only" ringing in your heart.

Endeavour always to be a credit to the Lord

As a believer there is an added incentive to do well. You do not wish to leave others with the memory of a Christian who would not work well. A bad testimony like this has to be avoided! Paul warned of such a possibility. When dealing with the question of work he states that the behaviour of a believer must be of such a quality "that the name of God and His doctrine be not blasphemed" (1 Tim 6.1). What is true of working life is true also of student life, because during these years that is your work.

Work, study, and live in such a way that no occasion is given to anyone to speak ill of the gospel and of the Saviour you represent. Endeavour always to be a credit to the Lord whom you profess to follow. Many of those with whom you rub shoulders will disappear from your life when student days are over. What impression will they take with them? Let it be memories of one who showed by example what it meant to be a Christian. In a world where there is confusion as to what a "Christian" really is, your fellow students will have seen the answer proclaimed to them in a living sermon which some may never forget.

A course in higher education or further education is not a honeymoon period from life. It is not a three or four year holiday. It is a testing ground and it is a training ground. In it may you study not only to gain the qualification you seek, but also to show yourself "approved unto God" (2 Tim 2.15). That will be a sound foundation on which to build for the years ahead and for whatever service you are called to do in your life.